THOUGHTS FOR THE SOUL

MERRILL PHILLIPS

Order this book online at www.trafford.com
or email orders@trafford.com

Most Trafford titles are also available at major online book retailers.

All scripture is from NKJV version of the Bible.

Printed in the United States of America.

ISBN: 978-1-4907-2627-4 (sc)
ISBN: 978-1-4907-2628-1 (e)

Trafford rev. 01/29/2014

www.trafford.com

North America & international
toll-free: 1 888 232 4444 (USA & Canada)
fax: 812 355 4082

CONTENTS

ETERNAL GUIDANCE SYSTEM

Proverbs 29:25

The fear of man brings a snare, but whoever trust in the Lord shall be safe.

Before the advent of modern navigational systems the compass was used by explorers and seafaring people as they traveled from one place to another.

Through the darkness of night or the depths of the deepest storms, the compass never deviates from pointing north.

Every time a mariner left the shelter of his homeport, he relied upon the compass to guide him back to the safety of a sheltered cove.

The compass was and is reliable under all circumstances and if followed one can go around the world without the fear of becoming lost.

As the compass is to those who travel from place to place, whether it is on land or sea, so is the Bible to those who follow Jesus Christ.

The Bible is the history of mankind, from his conception to the end of time. From its pages can be gleaned the promises of God. Properly applied the teachings of the Bible can guide us from birth to death. As the compass guides us physically, so does the Bible guide us spiritually.

The compass can be ignored, but in doing so, it puts the navigator in danger of disaster, so it is with the Bible, if one ignores the truths found in the Bible they are in danger of being separated from God for eternity.

Just as the compass always points north, so does the Bible always points to God. With the Bible in one hand and the compass in the other, we have no excuse for getting lost in this world or on our journey to eternal life.

CALLED

Romans 8:28

And we know that all things work together for the good of those who love God, and to those who are called according to His purpose.

Heavenly Father, we who have been called to serve Thee here on earth come before Thy throne with bowed heads and open hearts. We will endeavor to plant the seeds that will help lead the unrepentant soul to the foot of the cross.

For once so were we, we enjoyed and was satisfied with the sins that kept us from serving Thee. We could not see beyond our selfish ways. Father, it was not until we became restless and questioned our motives as to how we were living that we turned to Thee and asked You into our lives.

Even then, we had doubts if our lives would change, but with this request for change came the desire to be more like Your Son, Jesus Christ. For some it took more time than others to turn from our old ways and seek a new beginning.

Our old habits were hard to overcome, for Satan had promised prosperity and the fulfilling of our sensual desires if only we would follow him. At the time, we did not know any better. As the spark of freedom from the bondage of sin burst into an open flame, we became enthralled with the aspects of finally becoming a true disciple of Your doctrine.

Whether young or old was not as important as the fact that we did turn to Thee and was chosen to serve Thee. That was like the icing on the cake. From that moment on Father, we have striven to do Thy will according to our calling. We will neither look back nor regret our decision to open the door and ask You to come into our lives.

We praise You and thank You God for the opportunity to serve You, we expect nothing in return, for we know what we really deserve is eternal damnation, but instead through Your love You gave us the honor of serving You.

Until we meet You face to face, we will endeavor to be obedient children and will help our neighbor in their effort to change their lives as you have changed ours.

It is with joy in our hearts that we who have been called to serve God can say "God is real, He loves all and wants all to spend eternity with Him. Ask God into your life and be prepared for the greatest adventure that you will ever have in this life.

SOUL

Hebrews 10:39

But we are not of those who draw back to perdition, but of those who believe to the saving of the soul.

Dear God, when it is my time to leave this world may I stand in your presence.

May I glimpse into Your eyes and feel Your love within my soul.

Hold me O Lord, do not let me go, for once I was lost and You gave me life anew.

Thank you Lord for making me whole and washing me clean as the driven snow.

My soul rejoices as I walk the paths You have given me to trod.

I now know what it means to be born again and be free from the bondage of sin.

I once walked with my head hung low in shame, but now I walk with my head held high as I claim my rightful place by Your side.

The burdens that once kept me from You are now gone, they have been replaced with Your love.

What a joy to feel the warmth of Your love as I trod life's ways.

The sunset of life no longer holds the fear of death, the fear of death has been replaced with the anticipation of spending eternity with Thee.

FREE SPIRIT

John 8:36

Therefore, if the Son makes you free, you shall be free indeed.

The condition of the body has nothing to do with the spirit. There are many who have little or no control over their bodies. They are immobile and completely dependent upon others to help them with their daily needs. Their mind is not bound by their bodies, it is a free spirit, free to wander as far as the imagination will allow. As much as these people are prisoners within their own bodies and may find it difficult to communicate with others they reflect God and His love just as much if not more than most.

Jesus' thinking was so pure that when He looked at the afflicted, He never saw the affliction; He looked beyond it and saw the perfect person. Jesus rebuked the evil spirits and demons on many occasions and delivered many from their afflictions. Returning to their homes, they rejoiced and praised the Lord for their deliverance. As in the days when Jesus walked among us and healed the sick so does He today. Through prayer and supplication, Jesus is available twenty-four seven. He can and will heal us of today.

When you see someone who is a prisoner within himself or herself do not look upon them as being anything but what they are, a child of God and as such know the day will come when they will be free from their affliction, either in this life or the life to come. Be pleasant toward them, encourage them, this will lighten the burden they are carrying and give them courage to face life one day at a time. They have the same ambitions and desires that we all have.

Some of the most brilliant minds are trapped in a handicapped body, but that does not stop them from reflecting Jesus and following the plans that He has for their lives. In many ways, they are freer from the limitations of the body than a healthy person is. They concentrate on what they can do and do it well and are not like those who think that they have to do everything. They are also some of the happiest people that one can find. They do not see themselves as being handicapped, but rather see themselves as doing the best with what they have. They look beyond their disabilities and see things that most people cannot see. Their minds are not clouded with "I can't", but rather "I will try."

No one has a perfect body; all have handicaps of one kind or another. It is what we do about them that counts. Either we overcome them and learn to live with them or we succumb to them and let them ruin our lives. Happiness does not depend upon our physical condition; it depends entirely upon our relationship with Jesus Christ. True happiness comes from within, not our position in life. Some of the poorest people are often times happier than those with wealth.

LIKE JESUS

Ephesians 5:8

For you were once darkness, but now you are light in the Lord. Walk as children of light.

Dear Lord Jesus thank You for Your loving care, for Your sacrifice on the cross so that we might be free from the bondage of sin.

To do Your will in our lives, to be a ray of hope to those we encounter day by day.

To minister to our fellow workers in a way that they might be inspired to seek You and live a life more pleasing to You.

Instill in their hearts a desire to turn from temptation and replace it with a desire to walk in Your footsteps.

However, most of all that we might be as a shinning "Light" in the clouds of darkness and sin, a "Light" that others might follow into the sunlight of Your love.

Use us O Lord in whatever capacity that is pleasing to You, lead us O Lord and we will follow and give to you all of the honor and praise that others might direct towards us.

Loving Jesus, we come before Thy throne and ask that You guide us as we travel the road of life and grant that when this life is over that we might spend eternity in Your presence.

GOD'S LOVE AND CARE

Psalm 139:3,7

You comprehend my path and my lying down, and are acquainted with all my ways. Where can I go from Your Spirit? Or where can I flee from Your presence?

A gentle rain awoke me last night as it pitter-pattered on the roof. It watered the ground and washed the face of the flowers before forming rivulets and heading towards the sea.

Just as the rain watered God's creation, His love and care waters our soul and our body responds to its healing balm.

As the sun rose and warmed the earth, God's hand reached out and touched my heart and my life has never been the same.

Where once I chased the pot of gold at the end of the rainbow, I now seek God's love and care no matter where I go.

He now walks before me as I go through the trials of life and slowly I am being purified like fine gold.

He offers me shelter when Satan throws his fiery darts towards me and tries to entice me to follow him.

No matter where I go, whether it in the depths of the sea or the highest mountain, God prepares the way. Soaring high above the earth, I look down and see the grandeur of God's creation from the mountains to the sea.

In the bowels of the earth I might find myself and yet I am not alone, God is there keeping me from falling into the great abyss of sin.

God lights my path and steadies my hand as age takes its toll, I find myself seeking His love and care before his throne.

The love and care of God is to my soul as the rain is to the face of the earth and no matter where I roam, God is there.

I cannot escape this earth and dwell in heaven until I accept God's Son, Jesus Christ, as my Lord and Savior, this, the Bible tells me so.

It was through God's love that I was born and it will be through God's love that I will return to him when this earth I am through.

A TIME TO COME

Ecclesiastes 3:11

He has made everything beautiful in its time. Also he has put eternity in their hearts, except that no one can find out the works that God does from beginning to end.

I know not why God loves us just as we are. We have done much wrong and still He loves us and watches over us all. The days are short and the nights long, but His love endureth forever.

We may wander the world around but we will never find a love greater than the love God has for you and me. Human relationships we have many but the relationship God wants with us will outlast them all.

His love is so great that he sent his only Son, Jesus Christ, into the world to take our place on the cross at Calvary. There Jesus paid the price of your sins and mine as His blood drained from His veins and washed us white as snow.

From that day forward, our demeanor changed to include daily prayers to the one who set us free from the bondage of sin.

We now walk in His "Light" and when the occasion arises, we proclaim His word to all we meet on our road of life.

It brings joy to our heart ever time we bring his name to mind, not like the days of old when we used His name in vain.

This road of life is short and full of woe, but with asking Jesus to walk by our side we will fear not what is waiting for us on the other side.

When that day comes, we will enter into the glory of God and have all of our earthly questions answered in the wink of an eye.

There will no longer be any disease, sickness or death for we will be like Him and remember no more the heartaches of living here on earth.

O what joy there will be the day that we leave this old life behind and step through the door of death and awaken to a new life and walk with our Creator throughout eternity.

REPENT

Revelation 3;19

As many as I love, I rebuke and chasten. Therefore, be Zealous and repent.

As I was contemplating life one day the word came to me, "Repent my friend, repent while there is still time." I took this advice into my heart and wondered how it applied to me; to me it came again, "Repent my friend, repent while you still have time."

Needless to say I stopped that which I was doing and gave this matter my full attention. After much thought I concluded that God had given me another chance to turn from my wicked ways.

It was not easy at first to take this warning serious because the sins I was indulging in was pleasing to me and from my perspective they were not doing me any harm, besides that they satisfied my carnal desires.

How could my pleasures be so bad when they seemed so right, but deep within me the Holy Spirit had planted the seed to please God rather than myself. Slowly the desire to change became foremost in my mind, thoughts and deeds.

The first time I denied my sinful desires I had a strange feeling that I was doing what God wanted me to do and for the first time I felt good about what I was doing.

This feeling grew each time I denied myself and followed my inner feelings, which I knew was form the Holy Spirit, my life and life style changed in proportion to my growing faith in Jesus.

It became as I was told, "The more you listen and demonstrate God's ways the more you will want to please God rather than self." It seemed a strange way to live at first, but the more I followed that still small voice the more comfortable I became in proclaiming and spreading the word of God to those I met in my walk of life.

Today I look forward to and often go out of my way to reach out to those in need. To do otherwise now goes against what I have come to know as fulfilling the great commission, "Go unto all the world and spread My word."

Whether it is today or tomorrow start your journey to the foot of the cross, waste not the time you have here on earth, it is later than you think. No one knows when his or her time to leave this earth will come.

Through the studying of the Scriptures one can see the necessity to repent in order to gain the privilege of spending eternity in the presence of God, Jesus Christ and the Holy Spirit. This is the final goal of all who come to repentance and become faithful followers of our triune God.

UNWWORHTY AS WE ARE HE WILL SAVE US

1 Corinthians 6:9-11

Do you not know that the unrighteous will not inherit the kingdom of God? Do not be deceived, neither fornicators, nor idolaters, nor adulterers, nor homosexuals, nor sodomites, nor thieves, nor covetous, nor drunkards, nor revilers, nor extortioners, will inherit the kingdom of God. And such were some of you, but you were washed, but you were sanctified, but you were justified in the name of the Lord Jesus and by the Spirit of our God.

Without the love of Jesus Christ and the wisdom of the scriptures, all would lose their quest of eternal life. In all ways possible, Jesus laid out the pathway to life beyond the grave. He himself allowed his critics to put Him to death on a Roman cross. Through His death, burial, and resurrection Jesus proved beyond a shadow of doubt that there is life beyond the grave.

Jesus made it possible for all who come to repentance and accept Him as their Lord and Savior can enjoy eternal life. Free from all that now binds us to an earthly existence. All of this is free, all who turn to Jesus and allow Him to guide them through the maze of sin that tries to ensnare them and keep them from obtaining their goal of eternal life.

Jesus paid the price for your sins and mine while He hung on the cross of Calvary, He did not have to die the sacrificial death He endured. He did it out of love for every man, woman, and child that has or ever will live here on earth.

There is no greater love than what Jesus demonstrated that faithful day so many, many years ago, a love that has never been demonstrated before or since.

The sins of man are many; anything that goes against the teachings of the scriptures is sin. Man tries to justify his sins by claiming that he has the right to live as he pleases and that sin is in the eye of the beholder, therefore, there is no sin. Scripture clearly lays out what is sin and what is not. It is man who tries to justify and rationalize his sinful ways. As much as he tries, he is fooling himself and this he will find out when he stands before the judgment seat of God on his day of judgment. The argument for justifying sin is saying that God is wrong and I am right.

Once for all Jesus defeated Satan while hanging on the cross, we can neither add nor detract from that act of love, just by submitting to the will of Jesus Christ, we can enjoy the fruits of his sacrificial death. Peace, contentment, fulfillment, a sense of gratitude are but a few of the fruits we will enjoy when we leave self behind and become as one with Jesus Christ. This is not to say that we will not have any more problems, but that when we do face problems we will know where to turn for help to solve those problems.

NO OTHER CHOICE

1Peter 2:9,11

But you are a chosen generation, a royal priesthood, a holy nation, His own special people, that you may proclaim the praises of him who called you out of darkness into His marvelous light. Beloved I beg you as sojourners and pilgrims abstain from fleshly lusts which war against the soul.

It took faith to join hands and plan to leave ones native land and seek a new home in the wilderness of the New World.

The Pilgrims were driven by the desire of being able to worship God in a manner in which they were being denied in their native land.

To board a small ship and live in crowded conditions was not an easy decision to make, but it was either this or surrender their right to worship God as their hearts desired.

The desire to achieve freedom of worship was their driving force, for too long this desire had been suppressed. They were forced to meet in secret and risk being put to death.

They were willing to risk death at sea to accomplish their goal; death was more acceptable than living under the suppression of religious freedom.

Many times on their crossing of the North Atlantic, they probably had second thoughts, but it was too late to turn back, onward they sailed praying that God would see them through.

By God's divine hand, they landed way north of their intended destination and began a new life in what was to become known as Plymouth Plantation.

Also by God's divine hand, Squanto, a native Indian who had been captured by the British and taken to England where he was educated in the ways of England welcomed the Pilgrims and through his efforts learned how to survive in his native land.

Surly God was in charge of the entire situation, from the concept of leaving England to the establishing of Plymouth Plantation where they were finally free to worship God as their hearts directed.

Many gave their lives in their pursuit of freedom of worship, Just as we of today have struggled and died for the freedoms that we enjoy, among which is still the freedom to worship God in a manner in which we have become accustomed.

From these meager beginnings, our country has grown to what it is today, the most powerful nation on the face of the earth.

All to say, we as a nation under God's omnipotent hand has come a long ways from a small group of God fearing people who risked everything to gain the right to worship God in a manner becoming Him.

We as a nation have become as a "Light" set upon a hill for all to see that freedom of worship is worth all of the sacrifices that it has taken to establish and maintain that which the Pilgrims started so long ago.

GOD'S WORD CANNOT
BE SILENCED

Hebrews 4:12-13

For the word of God is living and powerful and sharper than any two edged sword, piercing even to the division of the soul and spirit, and of joints and marrow, and is a discerner of the thoughts and intents of the heart. And there is no creature hidden from His sight, but all things are naked and open to the eyes of Him to whom we must give account.

If God's word were to be silenced the stones of the earth would cry out and proclaim the word of God as being the truth and the only truth that can save man from destruction.

The word of God may be muffled, but those with ears to hear the word of God over the storms of life and obey what they hear shall overcome their trials, for in the end God cannot be silenced or denied.

Neither can the word of God be put in a box and listened to when it is convenient; for His word will so fill the box that the box will burst open and His word will come forth as a great flood and cover the whole earth.

The more God's word is suppressed the more it will spread, as in the past when His ward was suppressed the more it was sought after, the louder it became until it burst forth like the rising of the sun, it cannot be stopped or silenced.

The more man fights against the word of God the stronger it becomes, although during the times of war, God's word may be suppressed and spat upon, but in the end, it will prevail by reconciling the differences between enemies, with it will come peace.

God is patient, but the day will come when God will say, "Enough", and His word will bring justice to the whole world, all will receive their just rewards of how they lived their lives.

Those who lived by the word of God shall be with God for eternity, those who opposed the word of God shall be separated from God forever, alone, they shall suffer the rigors of hell.

God's word is like a soothing balm, it can heal all of man's problems without leaving even a trace of wrong doing or a scar to remind man of his wrong doing. God's word will flow like a river of living waters, bringing all nations together in peace and harmony. The past will be remembered no more, for God's word has declared it so.

NOW IS THE TIME

Ecclesiastes 9:12

For man also does not know his time; like fish taken in a cruel net, like birds caught in a snare, so the sons of men are snared in an evil time, when it falls suddenly upon them.

I know that I would have a greater walk with Thee O lord if only I would change my ways and give myself over to Thee.

Every time I try, pleasures of the past return and entice me to remain the same; they hold the promise of wealth and fame.

O Lord I love Thee but I find it hard to let go of the past and turn my life over to Thee, my sins offer pleasure, besides I am young and have time.

I know that I am on the road that leads to hell, but what am I to do? Every time I turn around there is another path that sparkles with the riches of this world and before I know it, I am hooked again. Looking to please myself rather than You.

Excuses are easy to make I know, like; when I am older I will have more free time that I can spend with You, but now I am too busy enjoying life and what it has to offer.

This is what the man said when he died and was cast into hell, "Lord allow me to go back and tell my family and friends to change now so that they will not end up like me."

To which the Lord replied, "While you were on earth I came to you and knocked on your door and you did not open it and invite Me in. Now it is too late to change your ways. Now you have eternity to regret your decision for not opening your door when I knocked. You turned Me away while you were on earth."

God added, "It grieves my heart to have to turn you away and cast you into hell. It was your decision to live life your way instead of turning your life over to Me and allowing Me to guide you through your trials of life. Now it is My decision for your unfaithfulness to cast you from My sight forever and ever."

FROM WITHIN

1Peter 5:6

For this reason, the gospel was preached also to those who are dead, that they might be judged according to men in the flesh, but live according to God in the spirit.

From within, there is a great desire to please God by allowing Him to express Himself through me. It is not a desire for self-gratification but rather a desire to humble myself before the throne of God and have His will fulfilled in my life.

Though it is a struggle to keep my thoughts and actions in line with Godly principles I strive towards that end and pray that God will grant me the wisdom and knowledge to fulfill my desire to please Him.

Self-discipline is one of the secrets to fulfilling my desire to please God, hard it is to keep from succumbing to the desires of the flesh, but this I must do. From the rising of the sun to the setting of the moon, Satan prowls around trying to entice me to sin, but from me he will flee when I turn to Jesus and use Him as my shield against him.

Most of the time I can overcome Satan's temptations, but occasionally I let my guard down and allow myself the fleshly pleasure of a sinful thought or deed. Satan knows my weaknesses and will if allowed bombard me with the desire to sin and forget that God is with me in all situations that I may encounter.

Pleasing God is my first priority, for to please myself without regard for God I am defeated before I start. This is when Satan tries to provoke me to follow my fleshly desires over the desires of God.

By filling my mind with Godly thoughts, I am able to overcome the overtures of Satan and keep my soul from being condemned to spending eternity separated from God, Jesus Christ and the Holy Spirit.

The goal of my life is to hear God say, "Well done my good and faithful servant." To give up the sinful pleasures of life in favor of obeying God is a small price to pay compared to being condemned to hell for a few minutes of pleasure in this sin-filled world.

Within me is where the battle against the temptations of sin rages. To let my guard down is to invite disaster, to stand firm in Jesus Christ as my shield and Savior ensures me of my rightful place in the kingdom of heaven when death overtakes me.

BITTERSWEET

Galatians 5:22-23

But the fruit of the Spirit is love, joy, peace, longsuffering, kindness, goodness, faithfulness, gentleness, self-control. Against such, there is no law.

This world is but a transient place, we are here but for a short while. Time enough to prepare ourselves for the next step in our existence and time enough to choose which path we will follow, the path of righteousness or the path of self-destruction.

A time to fill our pockets with the treasures of this world or a time to file our treasures in heaven. Either we will walk the straight and narrow path that leads to eternal life or we will go along with the crowd and end up in hell.

Christians learn to rely upon God for their needs while the non-Christian satisfies his or her lusts without regard for their fellowman.

Every sin we indulge in has its own sweetness and in the end its own bitterness. Along with sin, there are consequences that leave a bitterness in our mouths.

Just as each continent is an island unto itself, so is a Christian an island in the sea of sin.

Christians find this world bittersweet, looking forward to the love that awaits them on the other side of death's door. In the meantime, they strive to be as a "Light" set upon a hill.

Christians know that they have a sinful nature; therefore, they strive to overcome sin in their lives through Jesus Christ.

The blind (Spiritually blind) do not take sin seriously; therefore, they know not the boundaries of Christian living or fully comprehend the consequences of their sins until the day they stand before the judgment seat of God.

This life may be bittersweet, but the Christian has the promise of God that there is a better life coming when they leave this world behind and join their Triune God in heaven above.

BEWARE

Matthew 7:15-17

Beware of false prophets who come to you in sheep's clothing, but inwardly are ravenous wolves. You will know them by their fruits. Do men gather grapes from thorn-bushes or figs from thistles? Even so, every good tree bears good fruit, but a bad tee bears bad fruit.

It is the law of the land that no one shall mention the name of Jesus Christ while praying in any public gathering that is held on public property. Including schools, universities and any public gathering where federal monies support any part of that organization or meeting.

This travesty will one day come to haunt the conscience of those who have imposed their will upon the public, claiming separation of Church and State. It will not only haunt them but it will weigh heavy on their soul when they stand before the judgment seat of God.

They will find that their decision to deny Jesus Christ will result in Jesus Christ denying them before God. Resulting in their denial of being able to spend eternity in the presence of God. In simple words; those who deny Jesus Christ as the Son of God will suffer the fires of hell.

As found in the book of Matthew 10:32, 33, 38. Therefore, whoever confesses Me before men, him I will also confess before My Father who is in heaven. But, whoever denies Me before men, him I will also deny before My Father who is in heaven. And he who does not take his cross and follow Me is not worthy of Me.

No matter where we live in this world, Jesus Christ is the doorway to eternal life. Some may have never heard of Jesus Christ, but they have evidence of His authority and presence all around them, in the sky, in the landscape and in all that they see. Some of these will recognize that there is a higher power and be welcomed into the kingdom of God, while others will deny what they see and be condemned to hell.

Jesus would that all come to repentance and be saved. Jesus will not impose His will upon anyone and neither will anyone have an excuse for not knowing that there is a higher power than themselves, that higher power being Jesus Christ. It is by their own free will that people deny the deity of God's Son, Jesus Christ.

Would it not be prudent to accept Jesus Christ as the Son of God and avoid being denied before God? Who do you say Jesus Christ is? Beware, for the day fast approaches when one by one we will stand before the judgment seat of God and give an account of whether we accepted Jesus Christ or not.

LIFE IS A GREAT ADVENTURE

1 Corinthians 3:18-19

Let no one deceive himself, if any one among you seems to be wise in this age, let him become a fool that he may become wise. For the wisdom of this world is foolishness with God. For it is written, He catches the wise in their own craftiness.

Life is a great adventure and we can make of it whatever we please. We can follow Jesus and be saved, or we can ignore Him and live life as we please. The choice is yours and it is mine as to how we spend our lives, in the grace of God or in danger of being lost in hell forever. Jesus would that no one be lost, but he will not interfere in how we choose to live our lives or whom we choose to believe.

Jesus is loving and caring, but to hold us with fear is not His way. He extends love and a helping hand to all who turn to Him. Yes, Jesus loves us, each and every one, no matter our heritage or where we are from.

He will honor our decisions, good or bad and stand by us when we are sad. To reach Him all we have to do is bow our head and pray, "Come into my life Lord Jesus this day." Then leave the rest up to Him.

Jesus is faithful and keeps His promises, each and every one, He is not like us who runs and hides from what we do not understand.

Jesus created us to live here on earth in harmony, then sin got in the way and we left Him to chase other doctrines that seemed to say, "Follow me and I will grant your every wish if only you will leave Jesus behind." So goes the words of Satan. Then from nowhere Satan leaves us stranded in sin. Drowning in tears of sorrow, we begin to lament and pray for Jesus to help us work our way out of what we perceived to be the right way.

Once back on the road to eternal life Satan might attack us again, but this time we have the word of Jesus to keep us from falling again. Satan cannot stand before the word of Jesus and survive, from it he will run and hide and seek others who do not as yet know how to survive.

Yes, life is a great adventure, one that can be pleasant or one that can hold fear for those who turn the other way and chase the riches of this carnal world. The best advice any one can give is to cling to the teachings of Jesus and make Him the center of our lives. In return, Jesus will guide us on our road of life and set us free from the bondage of sin, making life a more pleasant adventure.

OUR MASTER'S HAND

Psalm 31: 15-16

My times are in Your hand, deliver me from the hand of my enemies, and from those who persecute me. Make Your face shine upon Your servant; save me for Your mercies sake.

One day this sin filled world we will have to leave. That is the day that we will drink of the water of life from our Master's hand. He will guide us and caress our fevered brow as He leads us from darkness into His "Light".

In His presence we will live for eternity providing we follow the path that Jesus laid out before us, by His hand we will be saved. Our evil deeds of the past will be remembered no more as we venture towards the "Light" that can save our souls.

The beauty and tranquility that we will behold beyond the grave will dazzle our eyes and fill our hearts with gratitude and love for the one who came to earth and paved the way to eternal life, Jesus Christ, the Son of God, our Master and Savior.

Once the choice is made to follow Jesus Christ look not back lest you stumble and fall and lose your way. Keep your eyes on Jesus while you hold His hand on your journey from life to eternal life.

Since the fall of Adam and Eve, man has struggled to discern good from evil, but struggle no more when you reach out and hold the Master's hand, the one who can save you from the rigors of hell.

The angels of heaven will join in songs of praise as one by one we walk through the gates of heaven and bend our knees before the throne of God and praise His Holy Name.

We will partake of the fruit of the tree of life and drink of the living waters that flow from the throne of God and live forever in the presence of our Creator and Master, Jesus Christ, the Son of God.

WHAT IF

Revelation 19:5

Then a voice came from the throne, saying, "Praise our God, all you His servants and those who fear Him, both small and great."

Where would we be if Jesus said, "I do not feel like it today, perhaps tomorrow?" What if He said, "The cross is more than I can bear, perhaps tomorrow?" Like all who procrastinate, perhaps tomorrow will never come.

It is with sadness to even think that Jesus could have refused to go to the cross and free us from the bondage of sin. Repenting of our sins would be useless without the sacrifice that Jesus made on the cross of Calvary.

Jesus was not forced to give His life as a sacrifice for our sins; He did it out of love for all mankind, by so doing He opened the door to heaven for all who come to believe in Him.

It may appear that Jesus lost control of His life and was crucified because of blaspheme against God by proclaiming that He was equal with God. In reality, Jesus is equal with God, for He was God incarnate on earth.

Jesus anguished over His forthcoming death in the Garden of Gethsemane, but once settled through prayer He gave His life for all the sins of the world.

What if Jesus chose to live a different life, where would we be today? Jesus had a higher mission, the mission of being a sacrifice for the sins of the world. He was and is the one and only Son of God, He carried out his mission of being a Sacrificial Lamb and the Savior for all who come to Him.

Honor Jesus by following His example; submit to His will as He submitted to the will of His Father, God. By reaching out as Jesus did we too can make a difference in the lives of our neighbors, whether next-door or half way around the earth.

We may not live to see the results of our efforts or receive credit for what we did, but by fulfilling the great commission we will have done what we were called to do. In humility we acknowledge that all honor, glory, and praise belongs to God.

What if God decided not to send Jesus into this sin-filled world on our behalf, where would we be today? Do not let "what ifs" control your life. Stand firm in Jesus Christ. It is a wise man who seeks Jesus and turns their problems over to Him to help them have a more fulfilling life.

COMFORT US

Psalm 23:4

Yea, though I walk through the valley of the shadow of death, I will fear no evil; for You are with me; Your rod and Your staff, they comfort me.

Comfort us O Lord as our bodies grow old and prepare to give up life.

Comfort us as we struggle with ailments of old age. Encourage us to carry on until the day of our demise.

Help us to see that this life is the time to prepare for life beyond the grave.

We who follow Thee pray that You will speak to those who have gone astray and guide them back to You.

It is with love in our hearts that we ask that You make our transition from this life to life beyond the grave a peaceful process.

Quiet our fear of death and comfort our soul as we go through the last stages of this life.

Even though we may know that we will spend eternity with You O Lord, we still harbor some sense of apprehension of the transition from this world to life beyond the grave.

Quiet these fears O Lord, so that we might come to Thee with open arms and a grateful heart, praising Thy name above all other names.

Grant us peace in our old age and courage to endure to the end of our days.

In the name of Thy Son, Jesus Christ, we pray.

LISTENING

John 15:12

This is My commandment, that you love one another as I have loved you.

Sitting by the oceans' edge, I laid back watching the clouds pass by, contemplating what God might say.

This is what I heard one day, "Come to me you who are burdened and heavy laden. Come to me and I will give you rest and comfort you."

"I will save you from the ravages of hell, if only you will obey what I have to say."

"Turn from your wicked ways, learn to love thy neighbor as thyself, trust Me, I know what is best for you."

"Apply My words to your life and you will have discernment to tell right from wrong, the knowledge to resist the temptations that bombard you each day."

"I will not force you to change; I gave you the freedom of choice, now the rest is up to you."

And then came the words that changed my life forever, "I love you and want you to spend eternity with Me."

These words burned deep within my heart as I lay by the ocean'
edge. By the time I left the beach that day, I was able to look at
the one next to me and see a child of God.

Where once I saw people who were displeasing to me now I
now see them as someone who was created in the image of God,
someone to reach out to in love, rather than with a critical eye.

Now when I am tempted to stray or criticize I think back to the
day that God spoke to me while on the beach I lay watching the
clouds pass by.

The day that God spoke to my heart and changed my life forever
with just the simple words, "I love you and want you to spend
eternity with Me."

CELEBRATE LIFE

Matthew 6:33

But seek first the kingdom of God and His righteousness, and all these things will be added to you.

O Lord as we pass from this life extend Your hand of comfort to those whom we leave behind.

That they might see the contentment on our face as we step from life to eternal life.

God knows everyone who belongs to Him; by their name, He calls them and holds them in His loving arms as from this life they flee.

From birth to death is a struggle indeed, but in His infinite wisdom God puts no more of a burden on anyone that they are not capable of enduring.

A time of testing if you will, to see how strong their faith is. To see if it is strong enough to carry them to the gates of heaven, instead of hell.

Many fall short and lose their way, but those who persevere and follow Jesus Christ through thick and thin will graduate from this life with flying colors.

Our days on earth are full of sorrow and woe, but once we step through the gates of heaven we are greeted with love and harmony.

God is to be praised every time a Christian leaves this live and joins their Lord and Master in heaven beyond the sight of man.

CLOSE TO MY GOD

Acts 16:30-31

And he brought them out and said, "Sirs, what must I do to be saved?" So they said, "Believe on the Lord Jesus Christ, and you will be saved, you and your household."

Close to You O Lord, that is where I want to be.

When things go wrong and I need comforting, I want to call upon You O Lord to chase my blues away.

At other times, I just want to praise You and pay tribute to You for all of the love that You have shown unto me.

Night or day will make no difference, I will testify as to how I asked You to come into my life and how You reached out and saved a wretch like me.

In days of old, I ignored You and did things my way, but now that You are in my life I listen to and obey everything You have to say.

What a difference You have made in my life precious Lord, I now go to Church and pray for the day that You will return so that I can live with you always.

O precious Lord what a day that will be, the clouds will gather in the East as never before and there You will be for the whole world to see.

You will stand in the clouds with Your pierced hands raised heavenward, the sheep of Your pasture will hear your voice and gather at Your pierced feet.

In robes of white, we will raise our voices as one, praising Your Holy Name, in Your presence we will be for eternity.

CAN IT BE SAID OF YOU

Ephesians 4:1

I, therefore, the prisoner of the Lord, beseech you to walk worthy of the calling with which you were called.

Have you done what you came to earth to do, or have you turned your head and left it to someone else to do?

Did God call you to do something for Him and you said, "Not me Lord, for I know not what to say or do."

Lest you forget it was God who created you, do not you think that you owe Him a thing or two.

As for me, I sure do, without Him I do not know what I would do. God loves us and wants us to know that all He wants is a chance to make His word to come to life through you and me.

Without you and me, He would not have a representative through which He can give a helping hand to those in need.

Put self aside and do what God has asked you to do, let not another day go by, for tomorrow you may die. Then when you stand before His throne, you will have to explain why you did not do what He called you to do.

Whatever your calling God will see that you will have all that you need to tell your story to those in need of what you have to say or do.

It will be a turning point in your life, a life that was once mundane will change into a life of servitude.

Serving God will brighten your days when you reach out beyond your family and friends; you will make a difference in the lives of those in need.

Hold not back from serving God, lest he cast you aside when this earth you leave, for as sure as you were born, one day God will call you home and then what would you do if you said "No".

God will not ask forever for you to serve Him, He will allow you to do as you please, but wouldn't it be better to serve God than hear Him say, "Sorry, you turned your head from Me, now I turn my head from you."

JESUS CHRIST

Hebrews 12:2

Looking unto Jesus, the author and finisher of our faith, who for the joy set before Him endured the cross, despising the shame, and has set down at the right hand of the throne of God.

J—Jesus came to earth through the womb of a virgin, whose name was Mary. His mission was to open the door to eternal life for all who come to believe.

E—Every day thank God for sending His Son, Jesus Christ to set us free from the bondage of sin.

S—Some reject Jesus Christ as Lord and Savior of all, but I say unto you that Jesus is who He claimed to be and without Him, all would be lost.

U—Unless you accept Jesus Christ as the Son of God you will not enter into the kingdom of God.

S—Someday Jesus shall return and establish His kingdom here on earth and then the end will be near.

C—Come, join me at the foot of the cross and receive forgiveness of your sins of the past, present and future.

H—Have you accepted Jesus Christ as your Lord and Savior? Do it now, for when you close your eyes in death it will be too late.

R—Read the Scriptures and apply God's word to your life and you will become as a "Light" set upon a hill.

I—It is important that all Christians spread the word of God at every opportunity, thus fulfilling the Great Commission.

T—Time is of the essence, Jesus Christ will return at any time, waste no more time, accept Jesus Christ as your Savior and inherit eternal life.

IN THE SHADOW OF THE CROSS

Matthew 10:38

And he who does not take his cross and follow after Me is not worthy of Me.

Because I live in the shadow of the cross, I have a tomorrow.

Yesterday is gone, tomorrow is my future and I will live it for the one who died in my place on the cross of Calvary.

Therein lays my gratitude, for Jesus nullified my sins as He gave His life for you and me.

O, how fortunate we are to have someone love us so much that He gave His life so that we might have a new tomorrow.

Only the Son of God could show that much love, my soul rejoices every time I pause and bring His name to mind.

Tomorrow, yes there will be a tomorrow for all who turn from their sinful ways, kneel before the cross, and accept Jesus Christ as Master of their soul.

Jesus' sacrifice on the cross has covered our sins of yesterday and brings us to a new tomorrow every day.

I can now see beyond my sins of today and will rejoice in a sin free tomorrow, one made possible by the one who gave His life so that you and I might live with Him forever on the other side of the grave.

His name is Jesus Christ, the Son of God, and the Savior of the world, the Messiah, the Lord of lords and King of kings.

In Him and through Him we shall live to see a new tomorrow, free from the sins that now bind us if only we will come to Him and live in the shadow of the cross.

LET JESUS HAVE HIS WAY

Hebrews 11:1

Now faith is the substance of things hoped for, the evidence of things not seen.

I live in the shadow of the cross because I turned my life over to Jesus and let Him have His way.

As He died on the cross of Calvary I was washed clean in His shed blood, now I am free from the sins that bound me.

Jesus took my sins upon Himself as his life ebbed from His earthly body; He died for you and me.

Never again will I have to fear what Satan can do to me, for my Lord and Master, Jesus Christ, rescued me.

By faith and faith alone, I walk the road of life with my Savior by my side, holding my hand from the womb to the grave.

The cross was the turning point in my life and it can be your turning point too, just turn your life over to Jesus and see.

Jesus is calling you just as He called me when on the cross He forgave us our sins and set us free.

To His Father's side He returned after Calvary, there He awaits for you and me, He showed us the way and still calls us of today.

Join me my friends and accept Jesus' sacrifice for your sins and see what a difference He can make in your life.

Come and live in the shadow of the cross along with me and we both will sing praises unto His Holy Name.

There is no other place we ought to be, it is the only place for me and I pray that you will join me.

As Jesus arose from the grave so can we if we live in the shadow of the cross and let Jesus have His way.

TOUCHED BY HIS MIGHTY HAND

Ephesians 5:8

For you were once darkness, but now you are light in the Lord, walk as children of light.

My life has been touched by Jesus Christ, because of it I will never be the same.

Where once I pursued the pleasures of life, I now dedicate my life to encouraging others to seek the protection of His mighty hand.

Jesus opened my eyes with loving care, now I can see beyond myself and reach out to those in need.

Dark clouds of sin once obstructed my view, now I can see the goodness in others and the way I ought to be.

When Jesus entered my life, He changed me from a lost sinner into a saint, a saint worthy to be called a child of God.

Before when I faced a trial I ran and hid from the truth, now I call upon Jesus and He comforts my soul and sees me through.

Whereas I was once under the shadow of sin, I now bask in the love of Jesus and see Him in my friends.

Jesus loved me enough to take my place on the cross of Calvary, there He paid the price of my sins and set me free to live for Him.

Yes, Jesus loves me, he loves you too, turn your life over to Him and see that which I tell you is true, you have everything to gain and nothing to lose.

With Jesus in our lives we can do all things, praise Jesus when things go right, praise Him when things go wrong and when in need and He will see us through.

Strive to spread His word through voice and deed to all you meet, you will never regret turning your life over to Jesus, for He is the only one who can keep us from going to hell when from this earth we leave.

Then we can stand up and shout, "I have been touched by the mighty hand of Jesus and my life has never been the same.

WITH JOY IN THINE HEART

John 15:11

These things I have spoken unto you, that My joy may remain in you, and that your joy may be full.

With joy in thine heart, sing praises unto God with all who gather at the foot of the cross.

With a melody of love in thine heart, sing praises unto the one who set you free. Sing of His love, sing of His sacrifice on the cross of Calvary.

Without Jesus, we would have nothing to sing about, so sing loud and clear, that all may hear.

From times of old to today, Jesus has been a "Light" unto our path and has filled our hearts with joy.

Sing joyfully unto the world, for God sent his Son, Jesus Christ into this sin-filled world so that we (you and I) might have life and have it more abundantly.

Sing praises unto God for allowing Jesus to open our eyes and see the sins of our ways, turn to Him and let it be.

Now is the time to turn to Jesus and seek His forgiveness while it is still day, for the night cometh when no man can see.

Glory unto God for sending His Son to be a sacrifice for your sins and mine, without His sacrifice surly we would be lost in sin forever.

Jesus' sacrifice at Calvary set us free, free to follow Him and live with Him for eternity, there is nothing more we need than to accept Jesus' sacrifice in order to be free.

Jesus is the only way that we can enter heaven when through the door of death we leave this world behind.

With praise on our lips and joy in our heart we go to the foot of the cross and accept the Lord of lords and King of kings (Jesus Christ) as our Savior and there, live forever, free from the sins that now bind us.

REPENT WHILE IT IS STILL TIME

Acts 2:38-39

Then Peter said to them, "Repent, and let every one of you be baptized in the name of Jesus Christ for the remission of sins; and you shall receive the gift of the Holy Spirit." "For the promise is to you and your children, and to all who are afar off, as many as the Lord our God will call."

At death, our flesh returns to the dust of the ground, our spirit returns to God.

According to how we lived, God will either welcome our spirit into His heavenly kingdom or disown us as we disowned Him.

God loves the unrepentant spirit, but He cannot look upon unrepentant sin, therefore the unrepentant sinner will be cast from His sight.

Death holds no fear for the true believer and they look forward to spending eternity with God, the lost of this world will resist death and curse the day that they were born.

The way of the cross is the road to eternal life, the way of the flesh is the way to eternal death, from which there is no return.

The choices we make now concerning Jesus Christ will determine our eternal destiny, if we choose not to repent then our future is very grave indeed.

Love for Jesus Christ and self-discipline can overcome fleshly desires and bring peace and contentment to the troubled soul.

Refusing to repent has only one end, losing one's place in the kingdom of God. It is not God's intent to cast one's spirit into outer darkness; it is man's decisions and choices that condemns himself to that fate.

To turn one's head from God and fall prey to the temptations of Satan spells disaster, disaster that can and will lead to separation from God for eternity and spending eternity tormented in the fires of hell.

Resisting Satan is a matter of putting on the full armor of God and allowing God to prevail in our lives, where God's truths prevail Satan cannot assail.

Repentance is a matter of putting God's will above our own, time is of the essence, death can come when least expected. Do not let death catch you unawares, repent while there is still time.

A TIME OF A NEW BEGINNING

Matthew 1:21

And she will bring forth a Son, and you shall call His name Jesus, for He will save his people from their sins.

Christmas is to be a joyous time of year in anticipation of our Lord Jesus' birth. a time of a new beginning, a time for a change of heart, to stand as one and proclaim our Savior's birth.

A time to forgive our enemies and reach out in Holy love, to do good to those who hold ill against us.

Christmas, a time when God came to earth in the form of a newborn babe. born in a lowly manger to a virgin by the name of Mary.

On that night so long ago, God sent His Son, Jesus Christ, to save mankind from their sins, a time to be born again and walk in the path of righteousness.

Christmas marks a new era in the lives of all who bend their knees before the throne of God and praise him for sending His Son as a sacrifice for the sins of the whole world.

Open your heart on this auspicious occasion and reach out to your fellowman in love, share with them the love of God and encourage them to take up their cross and follow Jesus Christ.

Christmas is more than a time to share with others; it is a time to make things right with God, by doing so you are giving back to

God the gift He wants most, that is you and your commitment to spread the good news of Jesus' birth.

Jesus is the reason for the Christmas season, come before Him as newborn babes and feed upon His word, then go forth and fulfill His command of taking His word to the whole world.

Be with and in Christ this coming Christmas season, He came to save you from the consequences of your sins and give you a new beginning. A beginning that will lead to the foot of the cross where you can receive the greatest Christmas gift of all, eternal life.

JUST FOR YOU AND ME

Hebrews 13:16

But do not forget to do good and to share, for with such sacrifices God is well pleased.

Jesus took our place on the cross at Calvary, to Him we owe. With love in His heart for sinners like you and me, He set us free.

Without hesitation Jesus stepped forward and took our sins upon himself and bore our penalty.

We owe Jesus a debt of gratitude, one that we can never repay without going to Him and offering ourselves in service to Him.

This is our calling, to let go of our earthly ties and serve Him wherever He directs us to go.

It is for us to take up our cross, follow Jesus, and let the rest of the world know that He is our Lord and Savior.

To die to self and serve Jesus is what we are called to do, our lives belong to Him and Him we ought to obey.

Tomorrow may be too late to surrender to Jesus; He calls us to surrender today while we still have the light of day.

Jesus took our place on the cross at Calvary, to Him we owe.

We will sing praises unto Jesus as we turn from our wicked ways and start our lives anew.

Our names are now written in the Lamb's Book of Life, this we know because Jesus promised that all who believe in Him shall inherit eternal life.

With such a promise go forth as children of the most high God and spread His word to all you meet on your road of life. As He gave to you and me, so give to others.

WHAT ARE YOU DOING FOR GOD

1 Corinthians 10:31

Therefore, whether you eat or drink, or whatever you do, do all to the glory of God.

Many of us go about our daily lives with little regard for our neighbors and sometimes with less regard for our spiritual life. We throw money at our social problems without becoming personally involved. Then we pat ourselves on our back for contributing our money to a worthy cause.

What if Jesus said, "I will pray the Father for you." and then left the rest of his mission here on earth up to someone else? Where would the world be today? Jesus came to earth to be a sacrifice for the sins of the whole world and He never deviated from His mission, even unto the cross at Calvary.

He healed many and continues to heal today, for Jesus spans all time and space. He gives hope to all generations to be able to achieve eternal life through Him.

Jesus trained twelve ordinary men to carry on after his crucifixion; they spread the word of God wherever they went, even unto death. Are we of today willing to do the same? Do we put God and his will before everything else? Jesus shouldered His responsibilities and never looked back. Few there are today who are willing to do the same.

No one before or since has showed such love towards mankind as Jesus did. Jesus gave his life for your sins and mine and asked nothing in return. No greater love has anyone than this.

Jesus left it up to each disciple as to whether they would follow His command to go unto the whole world and spread His word. His disciples were so inspired by Jesus' life, crucifixion and resurrection that they too gave their lives for the cause. How many of today would do the same?

It is up to each individual as to whether they are willing to become a follower of Jesus Christ and put their lives on the line for His cause. There are those who choose to do just that.

We hear of people around the world who practice the doctrine of Jesus Christ and are persecuted for their beliefs, even unto death. These are the true followers of Jesus Christ. They accept death rather than to deny Jesus. How do you stand on the issue and what are you doing to promote the kingdom of God here on earth?

A GREAT AWAKENING

Matthew 11:28

Come to Me, all who labor and are heavy laden and I will give you rest.

One day we will roam no more, our days on earth will have come to an end, great our comfort will be if we have accepted Jesus as our Lord and Savior.

Our eyes will no longer gaze upon His creation; our ears will no longer hear the cry of the wild, silent our world will be except for His voice that will guide us on our way to eternal life.

Our feet will no longer trod the path He laid out for us, we will no longer sail the great expanse of the seas, and treasures of old will no longer be.

Our souls will rest from the labors of this world, from death's door we cannot flee, some will mourn our passing, and others will smile and say, "O what a fool was he."

Our souls will rise from death, we will awaken to a new world, one not made by hands, and we will rest in Jesus' presence and forever be free from the temptations that now entice you and me.

We will not fear the day that we close our eyes in death, joyous will be our journey through the heavens on our way to eternity.

Our souls will shout with joy as the stars pass in review, at the end of our heavenly journey our eyes will gaze upon Thee.

Our road of life may have been long and arduous, but at its end, we will see the beauty of heaven pass in review.

We will regret not the time we now spend in Thy word, for it tells us what we need to know so that our soul might spend eternity with Jesus.

A new time, a new place, a new day awaits all who gives up self and follows Thee. From life to death to a great awakening, our souls will rejoice and forever be free from all that now keeps us from Thee.

PRAYER

Luke 11:1

In as much as many has taken in hand to set in order a narrative of those things which have been fulfilled among us.

God does not answer prayers on our timetable, for His ways are not our ways nor our ways His ways.

When praying take thy requests before the throne of God and leave them there. In His time and in His way He will answer them. Sometimes His answer will be no or He will answer them in a way that we least expect.

A prayer from the mouth can be likened to the wind, it goes where we know not, whereas a prayer from the heart goes directly to the throne of God and He in His infinite wisdom will answer that prayer in His way and time.

In answering prayers God is never early, nor is He ever late, His timing is always perfect.

A boastful man prays where others can hear him, a humble man prays in secret and he who hears in secret will honor that prayer.

Patience and self-discipline are virtues of a godly man, it avails him much on his journey in his prayer life.

Would you answer the prayers of a man who stomps his feet and demands that his prayers be answered and answered his way? This is a man who wants to use God as a means by which he can get his own way. This is also the man when he dies will hear God say, "I know thee not." and be cast into outer darkness, separated from God for eternity.

But the man who humbles himself before the throne of God and seeks forgiveness through prayer will be carried by the angels to the bosom of Abraham and be exalted before the throne of God.

Abuse prayer by praying for harm to others can and often times results in harm to one's self, be vigilant as to how you pray and what you pray for.

Prayer is the most powerful tool we have as we journey our road of life, use it wisely and we can accomplish much. One of the greatest prayers we can pray for is to have God's will fulfilled in our lives.

SEEK YE THE LORD

Deuteronomy 4:29

But from there you will seek the Lord your God, and you will find Him if you seek Him with all your heart and with all your soul.

God of the universe, Father of us all, Creator of all we observe, grant us peace and understanding.

Open the Scriptures to us so that we might have a greater understanding of Your ways.

Holy Father, grant us the courage and strength to go through the fires of this life as they eliminate the dross that keeps us from becoming more like You.

As we touch the lives of others, give unto us the wisdom and knowledge to influence them in a positive way. That our own lifestyle will be an incentive for them to want to seek You in good times as well as bad.

May we stand as a "Light" in the darkness of sin and be an inspiration to those less fortunate than ourselves.

Not that we are perfect or anywhere near it, but that we have a personal relationship with You O God and seek You when we ourselves are confronted with the temptations of Satan.

It is only through Your gift of strength and courage that we ourselves are able to overcome the adversities of this life.

We thank You O Lord for loving us so much that You sent your son, Jesus Christ, to take our place on the cross of Calvary. There, Jesus hesitated not to give His life as a sacrifice for the sins of the whole world and set us free from the bondage of sin.

Jesus, the one who provided us with a way to forgive our enemies and the ability to reach out to others with love that flows from your throne.

We, your followers humbly thank You Lord God for all of the love, guidance, and gifts that You shower upon us every day of our lives. Without You we would be hopelessly lost in sin. We seek Thee day and night and assign unto You all of the glory and honor that is due You.

These things we acknowledge in Thy Son's name, Jesus Christ, A-men.

THE TREE

Ecclesiastes 3:1

To everything there is a season, a time for every purpose under heaven.

The tree, a creation of God, all clothed in green, supplying man with many of his needs, from wood to build his home to the oxygen he breathes.

Birds of the air nest in the branches thereof, raising their young, hiding them from the predators who seek to devour them.

I stand in awe of the beauty of a tree, it takes my breath away, created by God, O what a magnificent sight to behold, a tree that reaches high into the sky.

From little seeds great trees grow, trees of all shapes and sizes forms the forest of this world, the home God created for man.

In the forest when a tree falls to the ground it returns to the soil from which it grew and supplies nourishment for the saplings that will take its place, that is the cycle of a tree.

In the spring when the weather warms the trees come to life and put on their new coats of green, many filling the air with the fragrance of their blooms.

During the heat of the summer the trees provide shade for those who rest beneath their branches, it does a tree proud to be of service to man.

As the summer heat gives way to the coolness of fall, many of the trees put on their display of brilliant colors, a time to wander through the forest and take in the beauty thereof.

After which the cold of winter sets in and puts the trees to sleep until the following spring, the cold winds blow as the snows pile high, changing the landscape into a winter wonderland.

A time to put on our snowshoes and cross the frozen lakes and follow the paths through the snow covered forest and when the day is done returning to the warmth of a cozy fire in the fireplace, sipping on warm mulled cider.

In the warmth of spring when the weather turns warm again, the seasons start all over again. God created it this way, and as for the tree, it will stay the same and be beneficial to man.

SUBMISSION

Psalm 55:22

Cast your burdens on the Lord, He shall sustain you; He shall never permit the righteous to be moved.

In a dream I saw Jesus standing on a far away hill, with arms extended heavenward He submitted to His Father's will.

What a sight to witness, my Savior doing what He had asked me to do, being a servant rather than a king.

With praises on my lips, prostrate I fell, asking forgiveness of my sins, I can see him still.

"Come unto Me all who are heavy laden, cast your burdens on Me and I will give thee peace." echoes across the valley of time.

Oh, what a peace I felt when Jesus lifted the burdens off my shoulders, a peace beyond understanding was now mine.

As Jesus had submitted to the will of His Father, so had I submitted to the will of Jesus and through this, I had found the peace that only Jesus can provide.

Heavenly Father, thank You for allowing me to dream of Jesus standing on a far away hill, doing what He has asked me to do, submitting to Your will.

This is one reason that I know that Jesus is who He claims to be, the Son of God, the Messiah, the Lord of lords and the King of kings.

Through casting my burdens upon my Lord and Savior, I have come to know the love that He has for all who bow before His throne and submit to His will.

BELIEVE IN JESUS

Romans 10:9

That if you confess with your mouth the Lord Jesus and believe in your heart that God has raised Him from the dead you will be saved.

Join those who believe that Jesus Christ is Lord of lords and King of kings and your life will never be the same.

From the moment you believe, your heart will be full of joy and you will proclaim that Jesus is now Captain of your life and keeper of your soul.

Your days will be brighter, and when in need you will go to your knees and consult the new Master of your life, from there he will lead.

Your eyes will sparkle every time you hear His name and before long you will be able to see beyond the clouds of sin that once blinded you.

The "Light" of Jesus will light up your life and to your neighbor you will proclaim, "Jesus has changed me from a sinner to a saint and if you would, join me please."

By the way you change and live will be a sure sign that you will not change your mind or follow the temptations that once dominated your life

Forgiveness of sin is yours now you have forgiven those who trespassed against you when in the secular world you spent all of your time.

All it takes is a moment of time to turn from your sins and seek the one who set you free when on the cross He hung at Calvary.

To Jesus we owe it all, to Him we pray when Satan tempts us to stray and indulge in sin that can keep us from our Savior's side.

Believe in Jesus and your life will change in the wink of an eye, praise Him for the love that He shows for you and me, leaving the secular world behind.

A VOICE ON THE WINDS OF TIME

Revelation 3:20

Behold, I stand at the door and knock, if anyone hears My voice and opens the door, I will come in to him and dine with him and he with Me.

Listen closely and you will hear on the winds of time a voice calling, "Come unto Me all who wish to live in the presence of God and Me for eternity."

"Come unto Me and I will show you the way; for I am the door that leads to eternal life."

"My Father gave unto Me the task of paying for your sins, gladly I gave My life on your behalf."

"Open your heart and let Me dwell therein, I will grant you a life worth living and I will supply your every need."

"You will receive the strength to resist the temptations of your world if only you will believe in me."

"The day fast approaches when I will return again, this time I will rule with an iron fist. Those who still resist will face the trials of the great tribulation, times my friend that you do not want to see."

These are the warnings and hopes that our Lord and Savior has towards all who live on this earth.

Listen to them and seek the one, who holds your very existence in the palm of His hand, he warns us for our own good.

Jesus wants to turn no on away, but unless we come before His throne with a repentant heart and a desire to worship Him, He will cast those aside who refuse to heed His warnings.

Jesus is all loving and tolerant, but He will not extend his protection to anyone who does not ask Him to come into his or her heart. He will never force Himself upon anyone.

Jesus' voice will continue to be heard on the winds of time, listen and you will hear his voice when you go to Him in prayer and ask directions for your life.

A HIGHER CALLING

Romans 11:29

For the gifts and calling of God are irrevocable.

It cannot be time for me to leave this body behind, for there is yet so much to do.

I will write for You and man too, if that is what is pleasing to You.

You have guided my pen through many a verse, happy am I that you chose me to transcribe your thoughts for all to read.

When I leave this life, they will stand as a mute testimony of Your love for man.

Pleasing it has been to be a servant of Yours, never wavering when in the middle of the night You woke me to pen a word or two.

I am at your beck and call O Lord; I love what You have called me to do.

Whether I live or die is not for me to say, it is Your decision O God when this life I will leave behind.

Old age is overtaking me, but deep inside I am as young as the flowers of spring.

Yes, I know the day is fast approaching when my pen will be silenced by a call higher than the one I follow now.

It may be today or it may be tomorrow, but whenever it comes, I will obey and look forward to serving you beyond the grave; for I know that one day, I must leave this world behind.

THREE OLD NAILS

Luke 23:33

And when they had come to the place called Calvary, there they crucified Him, and the criminals, one on the right hand and the other on the left.

The centurion went in search of some nails large enough to hold Jesus to the cross at Calvary.

He searched the town o'er and o'er, he finally found three old nails that he thought for sure could hold Jesus to the cross.

He picked them up, light they seemed, back to Calvary he trod.

On the way, those three old nails began to burden his soul, but on he trod and proceeded to nail Jesus to the cross.

Just before the ninth hour the sky grew dark, the lighting flashed while the thunder roared, the graves of the Saints were opened, and they rose from the dead and praised God's Holy name.

As Jesus hung upon that cross the veil of the temple ripped in two, from the top to the bottom it tore, exposing the Holy of Holies to all, not just a few.

The centurion was convicted of what he had done; he turned to Jesus and confessed his sin of buying those three old nails and nailing him to the cross at Calvary.

With this, the centurion was forgiven of his sin of nailing Jesus to the cross at Calvary.

Even though those three old nails held Jesus to the cross at Calvary, it was your sins and my sins that really held Jesus to the cross.

You see, no old nails, no matter how big could hold Jesus to the cross unless He was willing to give His life for you and me.

ONLY JESUS

Acts 2:31-32

He, foreseeing this, spoke concerning the resurrection of the Christ, that His soul was not left in Hades, nor did His flesh see corruption. This Jesus God was raised up, of which we are all witnesses.

Only Jesus could stand the brutality of the cross and triumph over the grave.

Only Jesus was strong enough to deliver Satan his final blow while on the cross He hung.

While on the cross that fatal day Jesus could have called upon the Angels of heaven and spared Himself the torture and shame.

But for His love for you and me Jesus kept silent and allowed man to put Him in His grave.

Knowing that it was the only way that He could return to his Father in heaven and prove that He was who He claimed to be.

Jesus came to earth meek and mild, did His appointed task in the shadow of the cross, was crucified and buried, but no earthly tomb could hold the Son of God.

Jesus arose triumphant over the grave and took his place by His Father's side.

One day Jesus shall return and all of the saint throughout the ages shall arise from their graves and stand with Jesus and be renewed.

This will also be the day that Jesus will separate the sheep from the goats and take His Church unto Himself, to live in a new world free of sin, disease, death, and shame.

Only Jesus has such power, glory what a day that will be for those who have come to believe.

DREAM ON

Acts 2:17

And it shall come to pass in the last days, says God, that I will pour out My Spirit on all flesh; your sons and your daughters shall prophesy, your young men shall see visions, your old men shall dream dreams.

I want to turn my dreams over to God and dream of His love he has for all. Dream of Jesus walking from village to village with His disciples by His side.

I want to dream about every word he had to say and let them penetrate my soul. What a thrill it would have been to walk with Him and talk with Him in those days of old.

When He healed the sick and drove the daemons away, I wish I had of been there to witness His love for their souls.

While I am dreaming, why not be one of His chosen twelve and really get to know Him and learn from Him while walking the dusty roads.

With the proper attitude I can be with Jesus every day, He has told me if I seek Him in my walk of life He will come to me and walk beside me.

He will heal me when I am sick and comfort me when I am sad, He will supply my every need if I seek Him in my mind, body and soul.

I can hear Him and talk with Him, if only I will read the Bible and believe what it says came from His lips. Lips that spoke and still speaks words of encouragement and truth to a sinner like me.

One day my days of dreaming will be over, my flesh will die, but my soul will flee this earth and stand before His throne.

If while on earth I prepared myself for such a day, I will triumph over the grave and hear Jesus say, "Well done good and faithful servant, come, spend eternity with Me."

Glory what a day that will be, the day that I leave this earth and stand by my Savior's side. This will be the day that my dreams will have come true.

FINALLY FREE

Romans 8:2

For the law of the Spirit of life in Christ Jesus has made me free for the law of sin and death.

The day that we die is the day that Satan will never tempt us again. Until that day, put your trust in God to give you the wisdom and strength to resist Satan's temptations.

If Satan does entice you to harm someone take it to God in prayer and use the truths of God as your shield, against which Satan cannot prevail.

God will protect us and guide us all our days if we use Him as our shield and buckler.

If we approach the throne of God with bowed heads and forgiveness in our hearts, He will forgive us our trespasses against Him and our neighbors.

One day we will be able to look back and see the love and guidance that God bestowed upon us, even when we were disobedient children, doing things our way.

The day of our death is the day that we will witness firsthand the freedom that awaits us beyond the grave.

Those we leave behind may grieve our passing but we will not remember the events that lead up to our demise. All things will be new, a new beginning, love in its purest form will be the order of the day.

Until that day, dwell in the knowledge that we have a refuge in the love that God showers us with on a daily basis.

Seek to live in peace with all, have a forgiving heart, spread the word of God by the way you live and conduct yourself.

Give thanks to Jesus for being the sacrificial Lamb for our sins and for taking our place on the cross at Calvary.

True freedom will one day be for those who now accept Jesus Christ as their Lord and Savior and as we pass from life to eternal life, Jesus will be there to welcome us.

CHANGED IN THE WINK OF AN EYE

1 Corinthians 15:51

Behold I tell you a mystery; we shall not all sleep, but we all shall be changed.

In the dark of the night as he slept, he saw the "Light" that set him free. Free from the sin that kept him from his Saviors side. Free he was before the sun did rise.

Rejoicing and praising Jesus Christ, he told his wife how Jesus had changed his life right before her eyes.

It was with gratitude that he testified to his neighbors of the power of the Almighty to change a life in the wink of an eye.

As time went on the Word he did spread whenever the Lord called him to write, without expectation of monetary rewards.

With joy in his heart and pen in his hand, he wrote not things of his own, but things that flowed from the throne of God.

The more he wrote the better he got, for God was training him to listen for the voice from within.

All of this took place late in his life, many a night God awoke him from his sleep and laid words on his heart to pen.

As he shared his offerings with his neighbors and friends, he came to realize that God had chosen him to spread His word to a hungry people who wanted to establish or reinforce their faith in God.

He found that helping others was all of the compensation he needed to carry on and help his neighbors grow in the Lord.

The best thing of all he maintained his humbleness as he often went before the Lord in prayer and gratitude for being called to write for the King of kings and Lord of lords.

BEYOND OUR SIGHT

John 14:2-3

In My Father's house there are many mansions; if it were not so, I would have told you, I go to prepare a place for you. And if I go and prepare a place for you, I will come again and receive you to Myself; that where I am, there you may be also.

Standing on a rocky crag overlooking the expanse of the open sea there is a future that we now cannot see. It may now be out of sight, but one day we will not only see it, we will walk its streets of gold.

A new home our Lord and Savior, Jesus Christ, created for you and for me just by speaking the word. Angels will guard its pearly gates and only allow the pure in heart to enter therein.

Never again, to be tempted by the serpent of old, the one who can tempt us with things pleasing to the flesh, including riches of silver and gold.

Jesus will be the "Light" thereof; there will be no more night nor day. The beauty thereof is beyond our imagination, but one day we will call it home. Friends, both old and new will hold hands and praise God and serve Him out of love and gratitude.

All of this may now be out of our reach, but we know that it is there, for the Bible makes it very clear that Jesus Christ has prepared a mansion for those who believe He is who He claims to be.

For now, we may be bound to this rocky crag we call earth and only dream of heaven and its beauty that lies beyond the grave. The day will come when we will walk and talk with Jesus as we hold His hand.

What is now beyond our sight will one day become reality. Jesus is calling, calling to you and calling to me to live a life that will one day allow us to join Him in paradise.

HE HEARS

Matthew 6:6

But you, when you pray, go into your room, and when you have shut your door, pray to your Father who is in the secret place; and your Father who sees in secret will reward you openly.

Jesus Christ, our Lord and Savior, hears our cries when we are in need. He hears our pleas whether from the mountains, the sea or the plains.

Jesus knows our every need and supplies them according to His will and in His time. He is never late and always on time.

Sometimes He tells us that everything will be all right, sometimes he tells us to be still and listen, other times He says no it is not the right for you, nor is it the right time, but answer us He will.

Jesus knows us so well and hears our every plea; never will He abandon us and leave us alone when we turn to Him in prayer.

Jesus loved us so much that He took our place on the cross of Calvary and paid the price of your sins and mine. His death was not in vain, for he set us free from the bondage of sin and opened the door to eternal life that faithful day so long ago.

He would that we come to Him with our needs, rather than accept them from the hand of Satan, who has only one thing in mind; distract us from following Jesus and losing our inheritance of eternal life.

Turn to Jesus when in need and He in return will hear us and supply our every need. Jesus' ear is attuned to our pleas; His answers may not please us, but He knows what is best for us and this my friend is all that we need.

BECOME A SERVANT

Matthew 25:21

His lord said to him, "Well done good and faithful servant; you were faithful over a few things, I will make your ruler over many things, enter into the joy of your Lord."

I come before you O Lord as a humble servant who is trying to find his way. I submit myself to Your will O Lord and let You have Your way.

All of my life I have had no special plans until you came into my life and encouraged me to submit to your will. From that moment on, I have been content in whatever circumstances I find myself.

Through the darkness of sin, I have wandered, which nearly lead to my demise, but Your love kept me alive.

At night the stars of heaven remind me of Your creative hand, You created the heavens under which I now stand. By day, the sun warms me as I stand before Thy throne and listen for Your voice to guide me and your healing hand to touch my soul.

I am Yours almighty God, Yours to do with as pleases You, guide me in the way that you want me to go. A servant I will be if that is what you want for me, just lay it on my heart where you want me to go and there I will be.

My days are growing short on this earth I know, but as long as I live I will be a faithful servant and await your return. Like all who serve You I too look forward to the day that you wave Your hand and sin will be no more, just Your love will remain.

Until that day I will be Your servant and kneel before Thy throne and pray for the forgiveness of my sins and listen for your voice to guide me the rest of the way.

FORGIVE

Matthew 6:12

And forgive us our debts, as we forgive our debtors.

The Lord is God; in His image, he created you and me. Pray that He created in us a forgiving heart and a tempered soul, one willing to forgive those who trespass against us.

Place within us O Lord the love that Your Son, Jesus Christ, displayed while on the cross of Calvary he hung.

Through all of the pain and suffering Jesus forgave us when He said, "Forgive them Father, for they know not what they do."

Yes, your sins and mine held Jesus to that cross that day at Calvary, the day that they crucified the Lamb of God.

Since then we have come to know His love and grace, when we turn to Him He forgives our sins and sets us back on the road to eternal life.

We can in some small way repay that love and forgiveness by forgiving those who have caused us pain and suffering.

Reach out with a forgiving heart the next time someone tries to entice you to sin, reach out with the love Jesus displayed when they drove those nails through His hands and feet that day at Calvary.

Forgive and forgiveness is the name of the game, join those who have turned their lives over to Jesus and gained a forgiving heart and a tempered soul.

Join in the prayer that Jesus will return soon and upon this earth, establish His kingdom, free we will be from the sins that now entice us. Forgive and be forgiven.

ALL ABOUT JESUS

1 Peter 4:8

And above all things have fervent love for one another, for love will cover a multitude of sins.

What can save a wretch like me, nothing but the love of Jesus? Jesus is a friend of mine, this I know because he gave his life for me on the cross at Calvary, there He set me free.

He now waits for me in heaven where He has prepared a place for me and when I die; I shall see Him and live again.

Without His love and forgiveness, I would not get to live with Him in heaven when this world I leave.

Yes, Jesus loves me, He is my Lord and Savior and to Him I owe a great debt of gratitude.

Unlike the days of old before Jesus was born, I have Him to turn to when things go wrong.

To Him I owe my life, every day I bow my head and give thanks to the one who saved me from the fires of hell, my Jesus.

When I die to heaven I will go and stand by His side, in the meantime he will guide me wherever He wants me to go.

Like an obedient child, I will obey His every command, night and day He will always be before me, encouraging me and loving me like the great lolving parent He has turned out to be.

With love in my heart and forgiveness in my soul, I will treat my neighbor as Jesus has treated me.

Thank You Jesus for being there for me, may my fellowman see in me the same love You have shown towards me.

Jesus' sacrifice on the cross at Calvary has set me free, free to pass on the story of how this life is all about Jesus.

NOW IS THE TIME

Luke 15:7

I say to you that likewise there will be more joy in heaven over one sinner who repents than over ninety nine just persons who need no repentance.

While living on earth we make the decisions that will determine our eternal destiny.

When we close our eyes in death, we will be on our way to a new life, one not now seen nor fully understood.

Depending on our lifestyle and our earthly deeds, we will either go to heaven or to hell.

Our choice to dwell with God will have already been made when we leave our earthly life behind.

No one can complain if they end up in hell, for by their own will they either obeyed or disobeyed the creator of all, God.

It is not God's will that we disobeyed, by our own self-righteousness we failed the task set before us.

We could not see beyond ourselves and our own little world around us, we shunned those who cried out, "Please help me, I am in need."

We went about our daily tasks and ignored those who were less fortunate than we.

Sinners we may be, but God still wants us to spend eternity with Him, so now is the time to change our ways and make amends.

Reach out to those around you who are in need, change your ways, come before the cross and lay your burdens at Jesus' feet, He in turn will lead you out of your life of sin and welcome you with open arms of love.

It's time to change, for once we close our eyes in death the die is cast, for we have already told God where we want to spend eternity by our actions and deeds while still on earth.

WITH THE STROKE OF A PEN

Ephesians 2:10

For we are His workmanship, created in Jesus Christ for good works, which God prepared beforehand that we should walk in them.

One of God's gifts to His children is the gift of writing. Fulfilling this gift is not only a calling, it can and does become a gift that is pleasurable for those whom God calls to serve Him.

In time, they come to paint a picture with words and express a feeling with the stroke of their pen.

They write of what comes to their heart and hesitates not to give all credit to God. The expressions that they wish to convey come easy when they open their heart to the will of God and allow Him to choose the words.

A called author need not know how to write or even spell, what he or she does have to have is a good relationship with God and the willingness to obey His will.

Following God's directions brings joy to the soul, a fulfilling that satisfies the longing of the heart.

To be the sculptor to a piece of art with words from the heart brings joy knowing that God is actually the author thereof and that you are just the one He chose to put it on paper.

Like one who whittles on a piece of wood until there is nothing left but the object that was inside that piece of wood all of the time. So it is with a called writer, they choose the words that forms a picture of what they are describing.

All who receive gifts from God will be the first to admit that without God, they can do nothing, but with God, they can do all things. Praise God for the gift you have, exercise it to its fullest and through it glorify God in all you do.

It is through the Holy Spirit that God works his wonders here on earth. If you have received a calling from God, hesitate not to fulfill that calling, for it will bring a peace and sense of fulfillment that you can get from nowhere else.

HIS BLESSING

Ezekiel 34:26

I will make them and the places all around My hill a blessing; and I will cause showers to come down in their season; there shall be showers of blessing.

I feel a warm glow deep inside, may the Lord's blessings be upon this house.

His love I feel when I lay this body to rest, protecting me while I sleep.

To sleep all night and rise to a rising sun is all I can ask, for some awake not, they have gone on to their heavenly rest.

As the beauty of spring breaks forth, I stroll down a wooded path, listening to my feathered friends as they wing from place to place.

Their songs of spring stir my soul and I too sing praises to the King of the universe, surly the Lord's blessings are on this place.

God has opened His floodgates and showered me with His love, this is all I need to fulfill my life, freely He has given, so freely I will give.

God has blessed me beyond my dreams, He sent His Son, Jesus Christ, to pay the penalty for my sins, and in return, I will spend the rest of my life serving Him.

It was God who created us, not we ourselves, when He blesses us it for us to pass those blessings on so that others might see God working in our lives.

Seeing, they may come to believe and turn from their wicked ways and become an example for those who will come after them. This is the way it was meant to be, passing blessings on from one generation to the next. May god's blessings be on those who come to believe.

Surly God's blessings are on those who seek to do His will, now and forevermore God's blessings will lead to life without end.

VICTORY

1 Corinthians 15: 57-58

But thanks be to God, who gives us the victory through our Lord Jesus Christ. Therefore, my beloved brethren, be steadfast, immoveable, always abounding in the work of the Lord, knowing that your labor is not in vain in the Lord.

The shepherds as they kept their flocks were the first to know that God in the form of man had come to earth through a virgin birth.

His name was Jesus, the great I Am, Emmanuel (God with us), Lord of lords and King of kings, so was Jesus born in a lowly manger.

He came to save the faithful from the wrath of Satan, He came so that we might have life and have it more abundantly, He came to be the door to eternal life.

Though Jesus was fully man, He was also fully God and held the powers of heaven in His hands.

He came to guide us on the road of righteousness, He expounded his Father' word, He loved all the same, even the most offensive person was the object of His love, He wanted all to come to repentance.

Jesus could have eliminated all evil and returned us to the Garden of Eden, but that was not in God's plan. He offered and still offers freedom from the bondage of sin, He left that decision up to each of us to decide for ourselves whether to follow Him or fall prey to Satan.

Jesus came to be a sacrifice for your sins and mine upon the cross of Calvary, there He defeated Satan and opened the door to eternal life.

His act of rising from the dead proved beyond any doubt that He was who He claimed to be, the one and only Son of God who came to earth to offer the treasures of heaven to all who follow him.

To stand for Jesus means willingness to give up one's dreams and ambitions for the advancement of God's kingdom here on earth in exchange for the promise of eternal life, which in itself is the greatest reward anyone could hope for.

Victory comes to all who forsake the ways of the world and hold to the promise of our Lord and Savior, Jesus Christ, when He said, "All who live by My words and follow Me shall inherit eternal life."

JUSES, MY LIGHTHOUSE

Psalm 27:1

The Lord is my light and my salvation; whom shall I fear? The Lord is the strength of my life; of whom shall I be afraid?

Jesus is my Lighthouse, His "Light" shines in the darkest crevices of my mind.

Whenever Satan tempts me, I turn my thoughts to a lighthouse on a lonely stretch of beach, its light piercing the darkest of nights.

It is in darkness that sin hides, Jesus' "Light" dispels that darkness and frees me from Satan's spell, how sweet it is to have Jesus to turn to when evil raises its ugly head.

At first sin is sweet in my mouth, but as time passes it becomes bitter, my soul can become tarnished and scared for life.

As my ship of life sailed through the darkness where sin hides I caught a glimpse of Jesus' "Light" shinning brighter than the sun that drives the darkness of night away.

His "Light" grew bigger and brighter as He approached me, not like the times I lost sight of the "Light" that could keep me from the Fowler's hand.

The scales of sin and darkness vanished as I was surrounded by the "Light" from my Lighthouse (Jesus), my soul was washed clean by the blood of the Lamb of God, all fear was gone as I rested in the "Light" of my Savior.

Now I know what it is like to be in the presence of Jesus, as I observed the "Light" that throws no shadows my soul was rejuvenated, I pleaded for Him to stay as His "Light" began to fade away.

At that point I was freed from my sins, not just one or two but all of my sins. Now I can face the problems of life with confidence and assurance that when I pass from this life I will spend eternity with my Lord and Savior, Creator of my soul, the Son of God, Jesus Christ.

Yes, Jesus is my Lighthouse, His "Light" will protect me all of the days of my life, He is my refuge and strength as I traverse my road of life here on earth.

HOPE

Psalm 37:3

Trust in the Lord, and do good, dwell in the land and feed on His faithfulness.

H—Have you turned your life over to Jesus? Time is getting short.

O—Open your heart to Jesus Christ and let Him live therein. Let His life be an example for your own.

P—Put your trust in the one who created you, Jesus Christ. He loves you and wants you to spend eternity with Him.

E—Every time you are tempted to sin, turn to Jesus and let Him be you defense against sin, Faithful is He.

AS YOU WERE GIVEN, NOW GIVE

Galatians 2:20

I have been crucified with Jesus Christ; it is no longer I who live, but Christ lives in me; and the life which I now live in the flesh I live by faith in the Son of God, who loved me and gave himself for me.

May God's love drift across this troubled land and soften the heart of turbulent man.

Many there are who do not believe, for they have rejected God's love and put their trust in things that rust and fade from view.

The things of this world are only for a season, those that are unseen are eternal and will never rust nor decay.

Those who put their trust in the things of this world and ignore God are blind; they know not that they have chosen the road that leads to hell.

Those who have chosen the doctrines that make them feel good and enjoy the moment are in for a big surprise when they stand before the judgment seat of God, they will inherit a whirlwind and never see God again.

Though this life may seem long, it will be as a fleeting moment when it comes to an end, then where will the unbeliever be?

Without Jesus Christ in their lives, they will pay the price for living life their way and when the end comes, they will be the first to complain.

On the other hand, the believer will not face the wrath of God when they die; they will be welcomed with open arms when through the gates of heaven they glide.

They will have paved the way here on earth by doing the will of God and turning from the deceitful ways of this world, they will have spent their time in service to God more than they were concerned about the things of the flesh.

As short, as this life is there is time enough to learn about God and His righteousness, time enough to set one's life aright and not have to fear their day of demise.

Now is the time to lay up treasures in heaven by doing God's will instead of thine own. Freely you were given now freely give to the one who gave His life for you, Jesus Christ.

JESUS, OUR LORD

Psalm 145:17-19

Deal bountifully with Your servant, that I may live and keep your word. Open my eye that I may see wondrous things from your law. I am a stranger in the earth; do not hide Your commandments from me.

The atonement for the remission of sin requires the shedding of blood. Our Lord and Savior, Jesus Christ came to earth and lived among us and while on the cross at Calvary He allowed His blood to be shed as an atonement for your sins and mine.

Holy Father, we acknowledge the sacrifice that your Son, Jesus Christ, made on the cross at Calvary on our behalf and for our benefit.

May His sacrifice burn deep within us and help us avoid the temptations that we are bombarded with each day of our lives.

We acknowledge that if it were not for Jesus' sacrifice on the cross on our behalf that we would not inherit the eternal life when we leave this world behind.

We also acknowledge that we of ourselves are not capable of achieving eternal life; we acknowledge that we fell from Your grace when we lived in the Garden of Eden and fell prey to the temptations of the evil one.

From that day forward we have sinned in Thy sight and in general have made a mess of our lives, we see not our own sins, for Satan has blinded us with his temptations of wealth, power, sex, and all else that is pleasing to the flesh.

Even though we may sin there is within us a deep desire to be free from the clutches of Satan and live a more Christ-like life, those of us who allow that desire to come to life will eventually turn from our wicked ways and turn our lives over to You.

The blood that Jesus shed on the cross so many years ago still has the power to save all who turn to Him and accept Him as their Lord and Savior.

Lord Jesus we pray for the strength to resist the temptations that leads to self-destruction, grant us peace as we go forward in our pursuit of eternal life. Help us to avoid the pitfalls of life, for You are our Lord and our Savior.

HELPING HAND

Matthew 5:15-16

Nor do they light a lamp and put it under a basket, but on a lamp stand, and it gives light to all who are in the house. Let your light shine before men, that they may see your good works and glorify your Father in heaven.

Heavenly Father, help us to put our personal feelings aside and join hands in love as we spread Your word wherever we go.

May Thy word sprout in the hearts of those who need it, may they find freedom from the sins that bind them.

We are all Your children even though some are lost and indulge in sins that separate them from You. Those who follow You willingly reach out to those in need and encourage them to change their ways.

This life is the time to prepare for eternity, the time to accept Jesus Christ as Lord and Savior, a time to reject the temptations of sin and cling to the teachings of the Holy Scriptures.

The righteous are praying for the end of Satan and his sinful ways, a time when they can live in harmony with their brothers and sisters in Christ.

A dream for today, a reality for tomorrow, for the day fast approaches when Jesus Christ shall return to this world and establish His kingdom here on earth.

In that day the clouds of sin will pass away and the Love of Jesus Christ will fill the hearts of all who come before His throne and submit to His will.

Be a helping hand to those you meet on the road of life, for once, you were lost and someone touched your life and helped you to become a follower of Jesus Christ. So reach out to others in their times of need.

GOD'S BLESSINGS

Colossians 1:16

For by Him all things were created that are in heaven and that are on earth, visible and invisible, whether thrones or dominions or principalities or powers, all things were created through Him and for him.

As I walk the highway of life touching the lives of those I meet, I pray for God to protect them from the blight of sin and bless them day and night.

As I sit by the seashore in the early morn watching God paint the eastern sky with shades of red as the rising sun pushes back the darkness of night, I ask God to bless the new day that is dawning.

Gentle breezes blowing from the mountaintops across the stretched out plains, stirring the grasses as they wave to and fro, like the palm branches of old acknowledging the sovereignty of God.

When the storm clouds gather and the thunder roars as the lighting flashes, even here God is in control, and when the storm is over God places his bow of many colors in the sky to show that his blessings are upon this place.

In a mountain steam, I bathe my tired and weary feet, lying on my back I watch in wonder as the clouds of heaven go scudding across an azure sky forming many different shapes.

Under the darken skies of night I stand in awe of the stars sparkling like diamonds, the full moon casting shadows across the meadows, surly God's blessings are on this place.

No matter where I roam I find God in every place, from the mountains high to the edge of the roaring sea, I see God everywhere. He showers me with His blessings morning, noon, and night.

I can never travel so far that I cannot see the hand of God going before me and blessing me as I journey through this life.

As God has blessed me may He bless you, when this life is over may we meet beyond the shadow of death and share the blessings that God has showered upon this place.